HANDEL
at the
Court of Kings

BY OPAL WHEELER

Illustrated by MARY GREENWALT

Zeezok
publishing
Elyria, OH

ISBN 10: 1-933573-03-1
ISBN 13: 978-1-933573-03-8

Published by:
Zeezok Publishing
PO Box 1960
Elyria OH 44036

www.Zeezok.com
1-800-749-1681

MUSIC

HANDEL AT THE COURT OF KINGS

CHAPTER ONE

IT WAS FAST growing late in wintry little Halle, and the low, thatched-roof cottages lining the crooked streets seemed to huddle more closely together to shut out the cutting wind and whirling snowflakes, driving in white clouds through the darkening village.

Old Anson, the crier, was covered from head to boots with the heavy flakes until he looked like a giant ghost, plodding along the winding roadway. Beating his hands to keep them warm, he called in a sing-song voice the news of the hour.

But tonight his bell sounded louder than usual and his voice had an anxious note, and hurrying to their frosty windows, the good neighbor-folk poked out their heads to listen.

"Sev-en o'clock and a little boy lost! Sev-en o'clock and a little boy lost!"

Putting down his unfinished boot, lame cobbler Nils hobbled to the doorway of his small shop.

"Bell ringer, what child then, is lost in Halle on such a night as this?"

"George, son of old Doctor Handel, gone these two hours past. Sev-en o'clock and a little boy lost!"

Wrapping their warm shawls snugly about their

shoulders, the good neighbors hurried to the big Schlamm House, just around the corner, where tall Doctor Handel stood at the window, his long hair falling over his fine white lace collar.

As he peered anxiously into the whirling storm, the heavy door was flung open, and Mother Handel and Aunt Anna burst into the room.

"We have searched everywhere, good husband, but the little one cannot be found," cried Frau Handel in alarm.

Aunt Anna shook her head sadly and a puzzled look came into her gentle eyes.

"So quickly it happened," she murmured. "There he was, walking quietly by my side, and the next moment, when I turned to him, he had vanished!"

Suddenly from the end of Nicolai Street came sounds of music and there, led by a flickering torch, a band of wandering singers moved slowly along, their feet keeping time to their music.

As they drew nearer the Schlamm House, Mother Handel leaned quickly toward the window.

"There he is — see — the little one bearing the light!"

Father Handel looked out sternly.

"What! The son of George Handel with a band of wandering singers? Surely it cannot be!"

Aunt Anna smiled to herself as she slipped away quietly. So the child had loved the music and run off with the band. Closing the door softly, she hurried to the snowy little figure.

"Come quickly, George. Your father is displeased with you for following the singers."

"No, Tante Anna — I must finish the song first."

With glowing cheeks and shining eyes, the small torch bearer went on with the melody until the very end, and the singers had moved on down the street.

Father Handel looked seriously into the bright, eager face of the six-year-old boy, his fair hair shining like gold in the light.

"They let me hold the torch, Father, and we sang for everyone in Halle! The music was beautiful!"

"Music! Music! Everything is music!" exclaimed Father Handel. "But it is not for you, my son. From this day on, let

me hear no more of it in this household."

The boy was dearer to him than anything else in all the world. He must have every care so that some day he would grow up to be a fine gentleman. Music was only for wandering minstrels, who begged for food and clothing at the house doors of the town. His son a wandering musician? Never! Quietly he turned to speak with Mother Dorothea.

"Wife, our boy thinks far too much of music and it will bring him no good. We must see to it that he thinks of more serious things, so that some day he may become a fine lawyer."

"Yes, good husband. But he is still very young and will soon forget about the music."

But as the days passed slowly by, George became more and more lonely, for the thing that he loved most of all had been taken from him. Patiently he waited for the evening to come, and just as the twilight faded into darkness, he ran to the high window to listen to the chimes in the tower near by, pealing their fine old chorales at the close of day. When the last sweet tones had faded into the night, he was happy again and went quietly off to bed.

And every morning early, as soon as the first ray of sun lighted his little room, he ran to find Aunt Anna, to beg her to walk in the streets with him, for everywhere in Halle there was music, and he wanted to hear all of it. And besides the singers, there was always the fine town band that played in the market square on special days of the week.

Creeping closer and closer to the men, George listened wide-eyed to the sounds that came from their long shining instruments. If only he might play on a horn some day, how happy he would be!

When Sunday morning came, Aunt Anna wakened him earlier than usual and together they crept through the dimly lighted streets to the church where he could hear the organ high in the loft. This was the best music of all, and when the tones rang out through the tall golden pipes, George sat on the edge of his seat, listening with all his might. How he longed to touch the black and white keys that made the great pipes speak!

But there was very little time to think about music, now that he was nearly seven, for the day soon came when he was ready to start to school. He stood before Father Handel, his coat neat and his fair hair brushed, ready to leave for the low wooden building across the village.

Father Handel looked into the bright blue eyes that sparkled up at him.

"Learn your lessons well, my son," he said gravely. "They will help you to become a fine lawyer some day."

George liked the lessons with his kind, patient teacher. But the best time of all was at the end of the long afternoon, when Schoolmaster Praetorious sat at his small spinet to play his simple melodies for the boys. George stood close to the master, eagerly watching his flying fingers as they raced over the keys.

One day, after he had finished playing, master Praetorious looked into the glowing face of his youngest pupil.

"Perhaps you would like to try the spinet, George."

His wish had come true! Breathlessly seating himself at the small instrument, he put his short fingers on the keys and soon had picked out a melody of an old song that he had often sung to himself. Schoolmaster Praetorious stood near by, watching his pupil closely. Ah, this young boy had talent for music!

Racing through the streets of the village, George could hardly reach the Schlamm House fast enough to tell Aunt Anna of his great adventure.

"If only I had a spinet, I could learn to play on it myself," he sighed longingly.

"Some day, perhaps," answered kind Aunt Anna, smiling as she thought of the little surprise that she had been keeping to herself all of these weeks.

The days went slowly by and George worked harder at his lessons, for if there were no mistakes, Master Praetorious would let him play on his spinet.

The sun shone brightly on the morning of his seventh birthday, waking George from a sound sleep. When he opened his eyes, there was Aunt Anna stealing softly through the doorway, a heavy bundle under her arm. Placing it carefully beside the bed, she lifted the cover.

"Joyous birthday, little one," she whispered smilingly.

"Tante Anna! A spinet for me!" gasped George, rubbing his eyes to make sure that he was not dreaming. Springing from his bed, he kneeled before the old worn instrument and quickly put his hands on the battered keys.

"No, no, George! You must not play now! Come, we will

take it where no one can hear."

Quietly they carried the little instrument up the long stairs to a far corner of the attic and carefully wound each string with thin strips of cloth, so that when the spinet was played, no sounds would reach the rooms far below.

There, it was finished at last! Breathlessly seating himself in an old armchair, George played his simple tunes over and over again. But there was all too little time and off he ran down the stairs to begin the tasks of the day.

And now, whenever there was a moment to spare, George hurried away to the dusty attic to spend happy hours at his beloved instrument. And even at night, long after everyone was asleep, he stole from his bed and crept up the steep stairs to learn the pieces in the big book that Schoolmaster Praetorious had loaned to him.

Many times there was no candle and he struggled in the dark to find the right keys. In the winter time it was cold and his fingers grew numb, but George did not mind. He was learning to play beautiful melodies!

Carefully Aunt Anna watched over him and when the hours rolled by and still he did not come to bed, she became anxious. Creeping up the long attic stairs, she peered through the darkness, and there was the young musician in the dim corner, bending over the little spinet as he struggled to read the notes of the difficult music.

"Come, little one. It is time that you were in bed and asleep."

"But the pieces are not yet finished, Tante Anna. Listen, and I will play for you," answered George softly, his eyes shining in the candle light.

Pulling her warm shawl closer about her shoulders, Aunt Anna seated herself on the cold stairs and listened in amazement to the lovely melodies, the delicate tinkling sounds stealing to the far corners of the old attic. How could it be that this boy was able to play such difficult music without help from anyone?

Her heart glowed with pride as she watched the small musician. Surely the boy would do something in the world some day, she said to herself.

One evening in early spring, when Aunt Anna had left the Schlamm House on an errand for Mother Dorothea, Father Handel walked through the house in search of his son.

"George! George!" he called through the long hallway. But there was no answer.

Lighting a candle, he mounted the stairs, but George could not be found. Suddenly he paused to listen. Surely he heard sounds overhead. Opening the low door, he climbed the stairs to the attic and there, under the low eaves, was his son, playing on a musical instrument!

"George!" The stern tones rang through the attic and the music stopped suddenly.

"I was just trying to play some of the pieces in the big book, Father."

"Music again! But it will bring you no good, my son, so the instrument must be done away with." And putting the spinet under his arm, Father Handel started toward the stairs.

"No, no, Father — the spinet is mine!" sobbed the small musician. "You must not take it from me!"

Father Handel looked at the trembling little figure before him. He could not bear to see the boy so sad, and putting down the candle, he set the instrument on the rough floor.

"Very well, my son. You shall keep the tinkling thing. But see to it that your noise does not disturb the peace of this household."

George was never so happy. The cold and the dim light bothered him no longer and he played to his heart's content. Many of the pieces were too difficult for his small hands, but each day he kept on trying until at last he had mastered them all. And now what fine concerts he gave Aunt Anna, making the old attic ring with his music!

One morning early, the Handel household was filled with busy preparations, for Father Handel was going on one of his journeys to the court of Saxe-Weissenfels, to care for his many patients awaiting him there. And this time he would have a little visit with Cousin George, who was valet to the Duke.

George watched eagerly. There was beautiful music at the royal court of Weissenfels! Quickly he ran to his father.

"Please, sir, take me to the palace with you. I will be no trouble at all."

Father Handel fastened the last strap securely.

"Another time, my son. But now I must be off, for it is fast growing late."

Climbing into the carriage, he set out on the narrow roadway, the horses' hoofs clattering briskly on the rough cobblestones as they began the long, forty-mile journey to the court of the Duke.

George watched sadly as the carriage jolted along the roadway. Weissenfels! Weissenfels! The finest orchestra in all the country round was at Weissenfels! Suddenly his face brightened and springing to his feet, George started down the roadway, running after the carriage with all his might. He must go to Weissenfels, too!

Faster and faster his short legs flew over the ground while he called after the carriage at the top of his voice. The burning rays of the sun poured down on him and the stones in the road cut into his feet. Clouds of dust blew into his face, choking and blinding him, and making him fall again and again.

Slowly the time passed by and on he struggled, never taking his eyes from the jolting carriage. At last it slowed down. Surely they would hear him now. Standing in the middle of the roadway, he called with all his might, but there was no answer to his cries.

The sun was high overhead when the horses stopped at the side of the road to rest. Now his chance had come! For a moment he stood still, and then with all his strength he cried out through the noonday heat:

"Father! Father! Wait — it's George!"

Was someone calling him in this lonely place? Slowly Father Handel turned to peer down the roadway. A child! He watched curiously as the dusty little figure plodded up to the carriage.

What was this? His own son! Doctor Handel could not believe his eyes.

"George!"

"Please, Father, please take me to Weissenfels with you," cried the weary traveler, his tears making clean pathways through the dust on his face.

Doctor Handel was sorely puzzled. What was to be done now? He had gone too far to send the boy back to Halle.

"You have behaved very badly, my son. But there is nothing left for me to do but to take you to Weissenfels with me."

"Oh thank you, Father! Thank you!" cried George, his eyes shining through his tears. "And I will be no trouble to you — no trouble at all." Curling himself up on the hard seat beside his father, he fell fast asleep and did not once awaken until the horses stopped at the court of the Duke of Weissenfels.

Sounds of music greeted them when they arrived at the palace, and there in the courtyard were the fine musicians, playing for the ruler on their instruments. George listened with all his might and wished that he might live here forever.

But there was all too little time to hear the music, for he was hurried off to the servants' quarters to bed, and was soon fast asleep, the sounds of the music ringing in his ears.

Early the next morning he was awakened by long trumpet calls outside his window and running to the courtyard, he watched the Duke and his courtiers ride off to the hunt on their coal-black chargers. Suddenly a voice sounded behind him.

"Ah, my fine young cousin, you are up with the sun," exclaimed the tall valet, laughingly. "But come with me, little early bird, you are just in time to visit the chapel."

Together they went through the finely carved doorway into the beautiful little church and there, high in the loft was the organist, practicing the music for a special service for the Duke. As the lovely compositions swelled through the chapel, George crept closer and closer to the big pipes.

When he had finished playing, Herr Körner turned to leave, and looking down, he spied the eager young admirer.

"So, little one — and you liked the music?"

"Oh yes, Herr Organist — you play very well, indeed."

Herr Körner laughed delightedly.

"Ah, my young man, then you shall be an organist now, too," he cried in fun, making room on the bench beside him.

Putting his hands on the keys, George began to play one of the pieces from the big book, while the organist listened in amazement. Word spread quickly throughout the court and one by one, the members of the orchestra stole into the chapel to watch the seven-year-old musician.

"An organist — and so young! He is surely a wonder child!" they exclaimed.

Every morning from then on, as Father Handel cared for the sick people of the court, George spent happy hours in the chapel, listening in wonder to the music of Herr Körner. And always there was a little time left for him to play, too.

Sunday morning dawned clear and cool and the bells from the old tower chimed through the courtyard, calling the noblemen to service. George crept quietly to his place beside Herr Körner. But now his friend was very busy and paid strict attention to his playing as noble lords and ladies in rich silks and velvets swept into the chapel.

Last of all came the Duke, ruler of Saxe-Weissenfels, his long jeweled cape sweeping behind him.

The solemn music began and George watched closely as the court organist played the long service. But when it was nearly ended, the music stopped suddenly, and motioning George to the seat beside him, Herr Körner whispered commandingly:

"Play, George — from here to the end."

With trembling hands, but without once stopping, George played the last difficult measures of the service without a mistake.

The Duke leaned forward in astonishment. What was this? A child organist in his chapel, and playing such music in perfect time?

"Bring the young musician to me at once!" he commanded.

George followed the solemn page through the long aisle and stood wonderingly before the proud ruler.

"Ah, my little organist, and who has taught you to play so well?" he asked kindly, smiling into the bright eager face before him.

"No one, Sire. I just taught myself on my spinet, in Halle."

The Duke was more astonished than ever and sent at once for Father Handel, who hurried to the chapel, to find George talking eagerly to the ruler and his courtiers!

"So, my good Doctor," said the Duke, "I have found your son, here, to have great talent for music."

"The boy finds pleasure in strumming, Your Highness. But music is not for him. My son will one day become a lawyer."

As he listened to the old doctor, the Duke became more and more serious.

"Herr Handel, I would gladly give all of my possessions for a gift as great as that of your son. I command you, sir, to see that this boy has the best possible training in music."

Turning to the delighted George, the Duke filled his small pocket with shining pieces of gold.

"And some day, my little man, you may return to live here at the court, and play in my orchestra," promised the ruler, patting the boy on the head.

George could hardly wait to get back to Halle to tell Mother Handel and Aunt Anna of his exciting adventures. His joyous voice rang through the room.

"And best of all, now I can learn all about music!"

Father Handel's quiet voice answered him at once.

"But you must remember, my son, that music will never be your life's work. It is only for wandering singers."

But the promise to the Duke must be strictly kept, and soon George was hard at work with the young organist and teacher, Herr Zachau, the finest musician in all the countryside.

George was delighted with the lessons on the harpsichord and the organ. And there was the study of composition, when he learned to write little pieces. Each week he surprised his teacher with music that he had composed, until there was no more room in the copy book.

But the young musician was not yet satisfied. He must have still more work to do.

"Very well, my industrious young pupil," declared Master Zachau. "Then we will start lessons on the violin and the oboe, and for them you can write new melodies."

As the months went quickly by, Herr Zachau became more and more amazed at the rapid progress of the small musician. Nothing seemed too hard for him. Even the violin, which is a difficult instrument to play, was easy for George, and after the long lesson was over, he hurried home

to go over the pieces again for Aunt Anna, who loved the concerts of the fine young player, drawing the bow so smoothly across the strings.

Sometimes, when his lessons at school were finished for the day, George liked to steal outside the city walls to the salt marshes with the neighbor boys. There, hidden in the long grasses, he could watch the six hundred workers, banded together in war-like tribes, battle with each other to see who would be the rulers of the marsh lands.

And there were the busy coal mines near by, where the men took him deep into the earth through mysterious dark tunnels to dig for the hard, black fuel. But best of all was

playing in the old castle behind his house, climbing to the high towers and hiding in dark, winding stairways, to pounce with loud cries upon the enemy.

But many times, as much as he liked to play with the neighbor boys, George would suddenly feel lonely, and hurrying home, he would quickly play his music and be happy again.

In the years that went swiftly by, he worked diligently with Master Zachau, who was so pleased with the work of his young pupil, that he tried in every way to help him.

Besides the long and difficult task of copying the works of the German and Italian composers, George spent many hours in writing pieces of his own. Already he had composed sonatas for the spinet and the oboe and violin.

This delightful little minuet that he wrote, you will surely want to play.

MINUET

(TRACK 1)

More than anything else, George liked to play on the organ. But the lessons with Master Zachau were never long enough, and always he begged to stay on in the church where he could be alone with the instrument. Then what fun it was to see in how many ways he could play the same piece of music, sending the melody thundering through the aisles!

One morning, after a long lesson, Master Zachau turned to his eleven-year-old pupil. "At last you are ready, George. Tomorrow you will take my place in the church and play for the early service."

"Oh, Master Zachau — if only I can play the music well enough!" cried the young organist. Turning at once to the instrument, he went over and over parts of the mass that he was to play on the following morning.

Early the next day, long before the sun was up, he hurried with Aunt Anna through the cold streets to the church.

"Now you will be the audience and I will play for you, Mistress Anna," cried the young organist, and seating himself on the high bench, he put his hands on the keys and the music swelled through the dimly lighted building.

One piece after another flowed through the great pipes and George forgot everything about him as he played on and on. The people, coming into the church, looked up in amazement to see the young boy, high in the organ loft, playing a concert at six o'clock in the morning. And what beautiful music it was!

Master Zachau, walking quietly through the tall doors, could not believe his ears. A concert at daybreak! He hurried to the organ to find his young pupil playing a sprightly dancing melody, his eyes glowing with delight.

"George! George!" he whispered. "It is time for the solemn mass. Find the music quickly and begin at once!"

"Yes, yes sir," answered the young musician, looking around in surprise at the well-filled church.

But there was no need to find the music, for George had learned it all by heart, and at once the solemn music began.

Master Zachau, seated on the bench below, watched in astonishment. To play this difficult music without once looking at the notes!

Yes, the time had come for the boy to listen to other masters of music, for he had taught him all that he knew. When the long service was over, he went again to the loft.

"I am well pleased with what you have done this day, my pupil. It is time, now, for you to travel to Berlin, where you will hear the great musicians and composers, Ariosti and Buononcini, who are playing at the royal court."

George could not believe the words that rang in his ears. To go to Berlin, the court of the proud rulers! But suddenly he grew serious.

"But my father, Herr Zachau — surely he will not allow me to go away from home to hear the great masters of music."

"I, too, have thought of that, my boy. We will go and speak to him at once."

Together they went through the streets to the Schlamm House and quietly Herr Zachau told his plan to Doctor Handel, who watched the eager face of his son as he listened to the earnest young master. Yes, perhaps the journey would

be good for the boy, who would learn at last that his music was only in fun.

"Very well, George. You may go to the court to hear the players. But you must return quickly and begin to work harder than ever at your studies, so that some day you may become a fine lawyer."

George was overjoyed at the good news and could hardly wait for the day to come when he would start off for the bustling city of Berlin, to hear the music of the noted masters at the royal Court of the Elector.

CHAPTER TWO

THE GOOD FOLK of Halle were still sound asleep in their snug thatched-roof houses, for the spring morning was dark and chill and not even a ray of sunlight had yet come to warm the narrow streets of the little village.

All but in the Handel household, where everyone was bustling with last-minute preparations, for soon it would be time for George to start off on his long journey to Berlin. He had been up since daybreak, dressed in his best red traveling coat. Now and then he rushed off to see if the coach had arrived, and hurried back to watch Aunt Anna as she busied herself in the warm kitchen, preparing a good hearty breakfast for her hungry family.

Just as George finished the last hot sausage, the clatter of horses' hoofs sounded on the sharp cobblestones outside.

"The coach is here, Mother!" he cried, running to the high window overlooking the street.

Yes, there was the carriage, drawn by four strong horses, and rushing from the doorway, George climbed into the front seat, calling a cheery good morning to jolly Herr Schlegel, the good friend of Father Handel, who was on his way to Berlin and had promised to take the boy with him.

Mother Handel, in her thick woolen shawl, hurried from the house with a large basket of lunch and handed it to the driver. Looking into the carriage to see that all was well, she smoothed the warm blanket at the back, and patting George on the head, smiled into the merry blue eyes.

"Be sure to stay close to Herr Schlegel, and do all that he bids you," she cautioned earnestly.

"And return to us quickly, my son," added Father Handel, looking into the glowing face of the boy whom he loved more than anything else in all the world.

With a crack of the whip they were off, and leaning from the window, George waved his bright scarf with all his might.

"Good-bye! Good-bye!" he called happily, as the horses rounded the corner and galloped onto the long, long road leading to Berlin.

Herr Schlegel looked solemnly at his excited young companion.

"So, my fine gentleman, and are you traveling far on this fine spring morning?" he asked jokingly, a merry twinkle in his eye.

"Oh no, Your Honor — just around the corner to Berlin," responded George quickly, and the two laughed heartily together.

Even though the windows were tightly closed, the sharp wind whistled its way through the cracks and it grew very cold in the carriage. But George did not mind. He was off on a great adventure—to hear the music of the celebrated masters, Ariosti and Buononcini, at the Court of the Elector.

Tapping a merry dance on the floor of the coach, he sang a jolly tune at the top of his voice, Herr Schlegel coming in now and then in his deep bass voice. On and on rumbled the happy travelers over the rough, muddy roads and at last, after ten long days of traveling, they arrived in the city of Berlin.

George looked eagerly around him. How tall the buildings were, and what crowds of people filled the streets!

But there could be no rest, for George could think of nothing but the music at the palace and before long he was on his way, and soon arrived at the splendid Court of the Elector, where a concert had already begun.

There, on a raised platform, were the ruler and the Electress with their royal guests, listening to the music of their noted composer, Buononcini.

George stood close to the door, his eyes wide with wonder. Never had he heard such playing before. The glorious compositions swept over him, filling him with the greatest joy, and when the last piece was ended, he joined heartily in the waves of applause and bravos that rang through the beautiful room.

Buononcini, in fine court costume of rich velvet and costly lace, bowed to the delighted people, and when the hall was quiet, he began to speak.

"Your Royal Highnesses, Lords and Ladies of the Court, I should like to challenge someone to a musical contest. If there is one among you who is ready to accept, let him take his place beside me now."

George looked eagerly about him, but there was deep silence. Was there no one to enter the contest? Then he, himself, must answer the challenge. Leaving his place quietly, he walked slowly to the front of the room and bowed to the astonished composer.

"I would like to enter the contest, sir."

Buononcini smiled with amusement at the young boy in dusty traveling costume.

"I trust that you are a musician, young man. But soon we shall see. Ariosti, here, will give us a theme and from it we will each compose a piece of music. I will begin and you will follow me."

From his place of honor, Ariosti played a difficult melody, and seating himself at the harpsichord, Buononcini wove a composition from the little theme. When he had finished, there was a round of applause from the excited audience. The dignified master bowed his thanks and turned to George.

"And now it is your turn, young man. Let us see what you can do with the theme."

The people leaned forward in their chairs to watch the small musician, seated at the beautiful instrument. In a moment his fingers were flying over the keys, one lovely variation after another weaving a magic spell over the vast audience.

The Electress Charlotte, herself a fine musician, eagerly watched the young player, his fair head shining in the light. Who was this lad with such rare talent? Surely he did not come from Berlin.

Buononcini listened angrily to the brilliant playing, a scowl of rage on his proud face. Someone had played a trick on him! Very well, then, he would teach this country boy a lesson that he would not soon forget. When the last variation thundered through the hall and cries of astonishment broke from the excited people, he turned sharply to the young musician.

"Ah, my brave stranger, I can see that you are a musician. But the contest has only begun. Tomorrow we shall meet again, when another test will be presented to you. Good day, young sir," and bowing stiffly, the master left the room.

Laughingly the Electress Charlotte turned to her royal guests.

"Poor Buononcini! He cannot bear a rival. Tomorrow we shall see some fine sport, for never will our great master allow the boy to surpass him."

Word of the power of the young George Handel sped quickly throughout the court, and on the following day,

long before the appointed hour, the hall was crowded to the doors with an excited audience, eager to catch the first glimpse of the boy musician.

Suddenly a long trumpet call sounded through the royal chamber and while the Elector and Electress with their royal courtiers took their places, the people stood to honor their good rulers.

George sat on the edge of his chair beside Ariosti, his cheeks flushed and his eyes bright as he watched the stately

procession, rich costumes and costly jewels shining under the crystal chandeliers. Soon he would be playing for this noble company!

At last all was quiet and from a side door came Buononcini, a pleased smile on his face. Under his arm he carried a large book, and bowing to the assembled company, he spoke solemnly.

"We are now ready to test the powers of the young man who played for us yesterday. Here in this book is a

composition that I have just composed. I assure you that not only will it test the powers of this young man, but it would challenge any living musician."

What could the music be? Curiously George sat at the harpsichord and opened the book. Before him was the most difficult composition that he had ever seen. It was a severe test, indeed!

Buononcini smiled as he watched the boy. Surely he would not even try to play the music.

Taking a deep breath, George sat up suddenly and the audience watched in astonishment as he began the long, difficult work. Soon his fingers were flying over the keys, and from the beginning until the end, he played the music without a single mistake.

The people were astounded and rising to their feet, their cheers rang through the great hall.

"Bravo, young musician! Bravo! Bravo!"

At once a royal page at his side commanded George to follow him, and in a moment, the young musician was standing before the rulers of Berlin, his fair head bowed low. In warm tones, the Elector spoke to him.

"Young man, you have pleased us all this day with your fine performance, and we would be glad if you would come here to live at the court, to play for us and for our royal guests."

George answered with a bright smile.

"Oh, thank you, Your Highness. But that could never be, for my father does not wish me to become a musician."

Princess Charlotte stamped her foot impatiently and her dark eyes flashed with displeasure.

"Boy, royal commands are meant to be obeyed. We will send word to your father at once."

A kindly smile lighted the face of the Elector.

"Young Handel, it would mean much to us to have you here. And we would send you to Italy, where you would study with the greatest masters, so that one day you would become the finest musician in all the world."

George listened in wonder. To spend the rest of his life in music! But that was too good to be true.

Word was sent by fastest messenger to Halle, and while he waited for an answer, George spent long, happy days at the court, where honors and costly presents were showered upon him by the members of the royal company.

But the best time of all was in the early morning, when, with a special guard beside him, he rode to the hunt on a coal-black charger. In the evening, after the fine dinner was over, he played for the royal family and the eager visitors who crowded to the concert hall to listen to the boy wonder. Already his fame had spread throughout Berlin, until the name of George Handel was spoken everywhere.

At last, one morning early, after he had returned from the hunt, word came from Father Handel ordering George home at once. Sadly putting his few belongings and his new treasures into the coach, he set out with Herr Schlegel, a heavy purse of gold from the royal rulers tucked safely away in his pocket.

The February snow filled all the roadways and it was bitterly cold in the carriage. As the horses stumbled on through the great drifts with their precious burden, George and Herr Schlegel told funny jokes and stories to pass away the long hours.

At last, after many weary days of traveling, the little roof tops of Halle could be seen, poking their heads out of the white mounds of snow.

"We are home, Herr Schlegel! Home! Home! Home!" shouted George. And leaping from the carriage he bounded into the warm Schlamm House. But Mother Handel hurried to meet him, her finger to her lips.

"Hush, George! Your father is very ill. He is waiting for you now."

Quietly George crept into the sick room and at once, a smile of joy lighted his father's face at sight of his beloved son.

"How good it is to see you safely home again, my boy! And to think that they might have made a musician of you!"

Very soon afterward, Father Handel died, and George was very sad. There was little money now and eagerly he set out to earn a living for Mother Handel, Aunt Anna, and the two little sisters.

At once he went to Master Zachau, who helped his pupil in every way that he could, arranging concerts for him to play at the homes of noble families, and letting the boy take his place at the organ in the church whenever he was away from Halle.

There was very little time for composing, but whenever there was a minute to spare, George wrote the melodies that poured into his mind and hurried with them to the master, who was delighted with the new compositions, especially this little minuet that perhaps you, too, can play.

MINUET

(TRACK 2)

Sometimes, when there were holidays at the Latin School, George called his classmates together and off they went to the Schlamm House for music.

"Play for us, George! Play for us!" cried the boys, opening the book of music on the clavier.

"Not until we have finished with the singing," declared the young master, handing the boys freshly written sheets of music that he had just composed.

Always the singers liked the new songs and sang them lustily. They were very proud of their young leader, even though he was very strict with them and scolded them soundly when they did not pay good attention. Sometimes, when they worked hard enough, George allowed them to sing in the little church on Sunday, when he was the organist for Herr Zachau.

In the years that went swiftly by, George grew to be a tall, handsome young man, loved by everyone in Halle. Now he was hard at work at the University, where some day he would become a lawyer, as Father Handel had wished. But always his mind was filled with melodies and he longed to spend all of his time in music.

Throughout the years, he had never stopped working with Master Zachau, and now he was a fine musician, indeed. Already he was known far beyond Halle for his playing and composing, and how happy he was when he was asked to give still more concerts at the homes of noblemen! Now he would be able to take even better care of his dear ones.

One Sunday morning, after he had finished playing the service in the church for Master Zachau, he turned to leave the organ loft and there, waiting for him, was a little band of solemn-faced men. The leader came to meet him.

"Herr Handel, we have been sent from the Council of Halle to ask you to accept the position of organist and choir director at the Cathedral for one year, for the sum that we have to offer you."

To have a real music position at last! George could hardly believe the words that rang in his ears. Breathlessly he gave his answer to the elders.

"Oh, thank you, sirs! I will be glad to accept your kind offer, and I hope that my services will please you."

He could hardly wait to reach home to tell of his good fortune, and rushing through the streets, he burst into the house, his heart pounding for joy.

"Mother! Aunt Anna! The most wonderful thing in the world has happened!"

The little family gathered around him in wonderment.

"Come, come, George!" laughed his mother. "Tell us what has happened."

"Good luck has come to us all! I am to be the organist and choir director in the Halle Cathedral!"

Mother Handel looked with pride at her tall, seventeen-year-old son.

"It is indeed good fortune that you bring to us, George, and well you deserve the honor that has come to you."

Faithful Aunt Anna smoothed her white apron, her cap nodding joyously, while the two younger sisters danced around the room, chanting solemnly:

> "George Frederic Han-del, Organist and Choir Master,
> Organist and Choir Master, George Frederic Han-del."

But there was hard work to be done before the next Sunday arrived, and every morning early, even before the sun was up, George hurried off to the Cathedral to spend hours at the organ.

It was cold in the stone church and very little light came from the high dim windows, but the practicing must be done, for all too soon it would be time to leave for his lessons at the University.

The week went swiftly by and when Sunday morning came, George awakened with a start. It must be time for the early service! Hurrying through the streets to the church, he looked anxiously about him.

Yes, all was in order, with the singers in their places, their costumes neat and the music ready. When the last chimes pealed from the old bell tower, the solemn leaders and the people of Halle entered the Cathedral, and putting his hands on the keys, George began to play.

As the stately music swelled through the church, the people listened in wonder, looking closely at the new young organist, sitting so straight and tall, high in the organ loft.

"Why — it is our own George Handel! And how well he plays — even better than Master Zachau!" they whispered to each other.

But George thought only of the music and watched the notes carefully, so that there would be no mistakes on this special morning. The boys of the choir followed their leader closely and sang the music that George had written for them so beautifully that the people were pleased, indeed.

Never before had they heard such lovely melody in their Cathedral, and they were happy that George Frederic

Handel was to be their director for many long months to come.

As the proud little family walked home together, George declared solemnly:

"From this day on, I will give up my studies at the University and spend the rest of my life in music."

"Perhaps it is well, my son," answered Mother Handel thoughtfully. "Surely you will know what is best for you to do."

There was a fine celebration dinner in the old Schlamm House, and when it was finished, George hurried into the little back room, for he was so joyous, he must put down the two delightful little French dances that had come into his mind.

And how you will enjoy playing this gavotte and passepied!

GAVOTTE
(TRACK 3)

PASSEPIED

(TRACK 4)

"There, finished at last!" exclaimed George, turning from the little spinet to find Aunt Anna waiting anxiously.

"And in time, too," laughed the happy cook, "or my fine supper for Master Handel would soon be finished!" And hurrying to the warm kitchen, she brought a steaming bowl of soup and hot crusty bread, fresh from the oven, for the hungry composer.

The months went quickly by, and even though his duties in the church became ever more difficult, George was never so happy, for all of his time was spent in music.

And besides his work in the Cathedral, he was asked to direct the music in all seven of the churches of Halle! This was a task, indeed, for special compositions must be written for each of them and soon there was not a moment to spare from early morning until late at night.

But at last the year came to an end and George was delighted when the leaders of the Cathedral came to tell him of the pleasure his music had given to the people of Halle.

"And we would like to have you stay on with us for still another year, Herr Handel, to direct the music in our churches."

George smiled happily at the honor that had come to him.

"Thank you, sirs, but I cannot go on with the work here, for I have decided to leave my home in Halle," he answered.

Mother Handel and Aunt Anna were much upset at the news.

"But there is nothing left for me here in Halle, for I have learned all that I can," explained George. "Now I must go to Hamburg and find something to do in that city of music."

Taking a small purse from her apron, Mother Handel put it into the hand of her son.

"There is very little money, my boy, but it will help you to live until you can find something to do. For long months now I have been saving it for just such a time as this."

George shook his head thoughtfully, and then slipped the little purse into his pocket.

"For a little time I will use it, but soon you shall have it back again, and with much more, besides."

It was not long before all was ready, and with a song in his heart, George started out in the coach in the crisp early morning, to seek his fortune in the great city of Hamburg.

CHAPTER THREE

THE SUN WAS high overhead when the old coach rattled into Hamburg. Clicketty-clack, clicketty-clack, rang the wheels on the rough streets, and pressing his face against the dingy window, George looked with glowing eyes at the bustling city.

Before the wheels had stopped turning, he sprang to the ground, sniffing the air hungrily to make sure that he was really in Hamburg, the city of adventure.

"Your bags, young traveler," called the driver in a sing-song voice. Then, looking sharply at George, he added quietly, "Pretty big place for a young man like you. Better have a look around and go back to Halle with me."

Looking up with a merry smile, George nodded brightly.

"Thank you, driver, but Hamburg is my home from now on."

Grasping his bundles firmly, he started happily down the street. What did it matter if he had little money in his pocket and knew no one in all the strange city? He was in Hamburg, where great adventures awaited him!

It was not long before he had found himself a small room, and carefully locking the door on his few possessions, he set out to explore the city of music. He had not gone far when his eye fell upon a small sign:

Wanted at once — Violinist for Orchestra
Opera House — Director Keiser.

A real position, and when he needed one so badly! Surely luck was with him. Hurrying back to his room, George seized his violin, and finding his way to the opera house, knocked gently on the door marked DIRECTOR. At once a brisk voice answered him.

"Yes, yes. Come in!"

The busy Herr Keiser looked up from his music writing, and seeing the violin case, nodded his bushy head.

"Then you are a violinist? Good. Come this afternoon, and if you can play the orchestra music, you may stay on with the men. Good day, young man."

George walked about the streets, his heart pounding for joy, and long before it was time, he was back again at the opera house and eagerly took his place with the men of the orchestra. And now if only he could play the music well enough! Carefully he watched the director and went through his part without a single mistake.

It was decided at once that he would stay on to play with the men, and George could hardly believe the good fortune that had come to him so quickly.

The men of the orchestra, who sat near him, were very kind to the new violinist and as the months went quickly by, they became very proud of the young musician from Halle.

George liked to play the tuneful melodies of the opera. And what fun it was to watch the singers on the stage, acting the story as they sang their parts. But when it was time to play, he paid the strictest attention to the music and did not once look up from the notes.

One afternoon, as he took his place in the orchestra, his eyes twinkled with mischief. He would play a little joke on his companions! As the conductor nodded his head and the music began, George stumbled in his part. Quickly the man at his side pointed to the place, but no sooner had he started again, than his bow fell to the floor.

Throughout the long rehearsal and for many days, George played badly, and at last the men became very annoyed and spoke to him crossly.

"What is wrong with you Handel? Have you forgotten how to play your instrument?"

George looked at them helplessly.

"Why, you see — the music was new — and so difficult!"

One day, not long afterward, the conductor was ill and

there was no one to lead the men. As the members of the orchestra began to put away their instruments, a sudden thought raced into George's mind, and walking swiftly to the front of the hall, he seated himself in the conductor's place at the clavichord.

Putting his hands on the keys, he played a sudden sharp chord, bringing the men to attention at once. With bright blue eyes flashing, he crisply gave his orders.

"Gentlemen, if you will follow me, I will lead you in this music. Now then, we will start at the beginning, and I will show you how I would like the score to be played."

The men of the orchestra were highly amused.

"The conductor from Halle! Now we shall have some sport!" they declared, laughingly.

But George paid no attention. Running his hands swiftly over the keys, he played parts of the difficult score with such ease that the men sat up in amazement. Surely they had made a great mistake, for this young man was a fine musician, indeed!

Taking up their instruments quickly, they followed their strict young leader closely. Again and again George stopped them to go over parts of the music and would not be satisfied until every note was perfect. The singers, too, worked harder than they had ever worked before, and when at last the long rehearsal was over, their cheers rang through the hall.

"Bravo, Conductor! Bravo, Handel!"

Of course he would lead the evening performance, as well, and eagerly he hurried back to the opera house, his shoes neatly polished and fresh ruffles in his dark blue coat.

When all was in readiness, the lights were lowered and George took his place at the clavichord. The audience leaned forward in surprise. A strange conductor—and so young! Slowly the lights came on the stage and as the curtain rose, the music began, the people listening closely.

Why, this young conductor was even better than their own Herr Keiser! The directors, too, were surprised and delighted, and as the audiences grew larger with each performance, they went to speak with the young leader.

"Handel, you have so pleased the people of Hamburg with your conducting, that we would like to offer you the position as leader of the opera for the rest of the year. We hope that you will accept, young man."

To be the conductor of the opera house in the great city of Hamburg! Breathlessly Handel gave his answer to the dignified directors.

"Oh, thank you, sirs. You have brought me great honor, and I will be glad to go on with the work."

The people of Hamburg were delighted with the fine musician from Halle and soon pupils made their way to his door, begging for lessons on the clavichord. And when the leaders of the church of the Magdalene came to him, asking him to be their organist and choir director, he was happier than ever and played on the organ with such power, that people came from far and near to hear the new musician.

One warm July day, as George sat high in the organ loft, busily practicing the music for the services, he heard footsteps in the church behind him and turning quickly, he saw a smiling, handsome young man coming to greet him.

"Handel, I am Mattheson, Johann Mattheson, and hearing your music in passing, I stopped in to listen."

Johann Mattheson, the brilliant singer and composer of Hamburg, known far and wide for his music! Eagerly the two young men talked together and soon they were playing on the organ, trying to outdo each other in making variations from the same little melody.

George made up this old French dance which he called "Gavotte with Variations." You must try to play it, too. And what fun you will have with the variations!

GAVOTTE WITH VARIATIONS
(TRACK 5)

Variation

The two young musicians became close friends, and to his own home and the homes of all the noted musicians in the city, Johann took his new friend, George, who played everywhere on the clavichord, astounding everyone who heard him.

One bright morning, as George sat in his little room, Mattheson burst in upon him, calling merrily,

"An adventure awaits us, my dear Handel. Word has just come from Lübeck, of a fine organ position there. Shall we try our luck, my friend?"

"At once! On to Lübeck!" cried Handel, gaily, and down the street raced the adventurers, catching the ricketty post just in time.

Soon they were jogging over the bumpy roads, laughing and talking merrily together. When at last they arrived in

Lübeck, they went at once to the Marienkirche where the director, Herr Wedderkopp, in shiny black coat, looked at them sharply over his spectacles.

"Handel and Mattheson, from Hamburg. Yes, yes, I have heard of your playing, young sirs. Our great organist, Buxtehude, is fast growing old, and someone must soon take his place. Now then, I will be glad to listen while you perform at the instrument."

As the noble music rang through the church, Herr Wedderkopp became more and more excited. If only Buxtehude, himself, could be here to listen to these fine musicians! Nodding and smiling with pleasure, the short little director hurried to the organists.

"Young gentlemen, you have won the position equally. But as we cannot use two organists, whichever of you is willing to marry the daughter of Buxtehude, he shall be given the post."

To marry the daughter of Buxtehude! Helplessly the organists looked at each other and at last Handel answered the director seriously.

"Thank you, Herr Wedderkopp, but we must have time to consider your bargain. Good day to you, sir."

Leaving the church, the astonished musicians left Lübeck with all possible speed, breathing happy sighs as the city of Hamburg came into view. Handel was so glad to be safely at home again, that he sat at his desk to write this delightful gavotte, which is an old French dance, and one that you, too, may be able to play.

GAVOTTE
(TRACK 6)

One evening, as George was on his way home, still humming melodies from the opera that he had just conducted, he stopped suddenly under an old street lamp as an idea came to him. He had been conducting operas written by other composers. Why should he not write an opera of his own? Surely it would do no harm to try.

Almost at once, melodies began to pour into his mind, and scarcely could he get home fast enough to put them down. From then on, whenever there was a moment to spare, he worked with all his might and in a few short weeks, the new opera, "Almira," was finished. His first opera — at twenty!

He could hardly wait to show the freshly written sheets to Mattheson.

"But Handel, this is a beautiful work!" cried his friend, humming bits of the music. "We must produce it at once!"

George smiled happily.

"And you, my friend, will sing the leading part!"

Joyously they left for the opera house and on the very next day the rehearsals began. In just one week, "Almira" was ready, and breathlessly Handel watched the audience slowly enter the hall, ready to listen to his new opera!

The music began and the people watched eagerly as the beautiful work went on. Why, this was a fine opera, indeed, and written by their own young conductor! When the curtain went down and the applause rained upon him, Handel turned to face the excited audience, bowing his thanks again and again.

For many nights George conducted his new work for the delighted people of Hamburg, until time for the opera house to close.

And now he was free to play in concerts and George spent many happy evenings with the finest musicians in Hamburg. He was now the leading harpsichord player in all the city, and wherever he performed, the Italian Prince Medici went to hear him, and the two became good friends.

Prince Medici played with great skill on the flute, and George loved to listen to the liquid notes rippling from the shining silver pipe. One evening, after the last delicate tones had died away, he turned with glowing eyes to his friend.

"The music was beautiful, Prince Medici!"

"Ah, my good Handel, from such a great musician, that is praise, indeed. And each time that I hear your music, I long to have you share your playing with the people of my country. Why not go to Italy for a little visit, my friend?"

"Some day, perhaps," answered George quietly, "for I have wished to go to your beautiful country for many long years."

Italy — land of music and merry-hearted people! All that night George dreamed of nothing else, and when the dawn stole in at the window, he awoke, resolved to start off as soon as possible. In a short time all was arranged, and joyously packing a few belongings, George hastily boarded the post and clattered away from Hamburg. At last he was on his way to Italy!

When he arrived in Florence, the beautiful City of Flowers, he went at once to the fine palace of the royal Prince Ferdinand, who greeted him warmly.

"My brother in Hamburg has told me of your coming and I am glad to welcome you to our country, Herr Handel. If you are not over-weary with journeying, I should be happy if you would play for my guests." At once the dusty traveler was led to a fine suite of rooms overlooking a stately garden, with long lines of cypress trees and masses of delicate blooms. It was all like a beautiful dream.

Suddenly there was a low knock on the door and a servant entered, bearing a gift from the prince — a fine costume of deep red velvet, richly embroidered in gold, with hand-wrought shoe buckles of shining silver! Hurriedly dressing himself in the handsome court dress, Handel made his way down the great staircase to the music room, lighted by glistening crystal chandeliers.

At once, a page in scarlet uniform announced the guest to the royal company.

"Prince Ferdinand presents to you with pleasure, the noted composer, George Frederic Handel."

As George took his place at the beautiful clavichord, sitting straight and tall and with head erect, all eyes were upon him. This handsome young man looked like a royal prince, indeed.

But in a moment, George had forgotten everything but his music, and running his fingers lightly over the keys, he began to play this little gigue that he had composed.

Can you play the music, too, and in a lively manner?

GIGUE

(TRACK 7)

90

As the music went on, a rustle of excitement passed over the assembled company, and as the playing became ever more brilliant, the audience could be still no longer, and broke into excited applause.

"Bravo, Saxon! Bravo! Bravo!"

There was all of Italy yet to be seen, and in a few days George said good-bye to the kind prince and eagerly made his way to Rome and Venice, playing on the organ in the churches there, astounding all who came to hear him. Soon his fame had spread far and wide and the name of Handel was spoken everywhere.

One evening, as the moon flooded the long canals of Venice with silvery light, George drifted along in a gondola, enjoying the singing of the old gondolier behind him, when suddenly they came to a palace. There, under the soft lights, crowds of merrymakers were dancing on the highly polished floors, their laughing eyes hidden by narrow black masks.

He must get closer to the music, and stepping ashore, Handel stood on the palace steps, eagerly watching the bright whirling costumes and listening to the tuneful melodies.

Suddenly the music stopped and in the long pause that followed, a tall masked figure moved slowly through the ballroom to the harpsichord, and seating himself, began to play.

Strong, ringing chords startled the merrymakers and at once they crowded around to listen. Then came swiftly running passages, the fingers of the player racing over the keys with such power that the excited revelers broke into a round of applause.

"Bravo, Stranger! Bravo, Musician!"

The handsome young Scarlatti, noted Italian composer, was startled at the sounds. Who was this man, playing as no one in Italy had ever played before? Pushing his way through the crowd, he grasped the shoulder of the stranger, crying,

"You are either the Saxon or the Devil! Unmask, sir!"

With delighted cries, the crowd pressed closer, and pulling the black cloth from his eyes, Handel laughed merrily.

"The Saxon! The Saxon!" cried the revelers, and would not go on with their dancing until he had played for them again.

From that moment on, Handel and Scarlatti became close friends, traveling from one lovely Italian city to another, giving concerts, conducting, and composing. With so much music everywhere, the melodies would not stop coming, and cantatas, songs, pieces for instruments, and an opera, came from Handel's pen.

This delightful vivace of his you will want to try at once.

VIVACE
(TRACK 8)

Everywhere gifts and honors were showered upon Handel and his name rang through the countryside. If only he could stay forever in this land of music! But he must earn his living, and all the fame and honor in Italy would not do that for him.

There were many times now when he went without food to save the little money that was left, and sadly he knew that there was nothing left for him to do but to go back to Hamburg and begin the dreary work of teaching his pupils there.

One evening in Venice, when he was conducting his opera for the last time, the Prince of Hanover, seated in a box near the stage, leaned forward in keen interest. Here was a fine musician, indeed — and a composer, as well! He must speak to this young man at once.

When the curtain was lowered and the last beautiful melody had been played for the delighted audience, the Prince sent his special messenger to the stage, asking Handel to speak with him in his box. In a few moments, the happy composer stood before the proud ruler.

"Your conducting has pleased me very much, Herr Handel. I would be glad if you would return to Hanover with me to take charge of the music at my court."

Handel's eyes brightened with pleasure. This would be a new adventure, and besides, he would have a real position, when he needed one so badly.

"Thank you, Your Highness," he answered, bowing low. "I will be glad to accept your kind offer."

Bidding good-bye to his kind friend, Scarlatti, Handel left for the royal court of the Prince, where he was soon at work directing the fine group of players, who eagerly followed their strict young conductor.

But as the months went slowly by, a great longing came over Handel to go traveling again. He would like to go to England, for many invitations had come to him from the people there, asking him to play for them in their country. There was only one thing for him to do. He must speak to the Prince at once.

"Your Highness, I beg permission to leave the court for a little time, for I must go to England."

"England!" exclaimed the Prince, his wig trembling with anger as he rapped on the ground with his gold-headed cane. "But I cannot spare you, Handel. There is no one now but you, who can please me with music."

Then, looking sharply into the determined blue eyes of his young conductor, the Prince nodded slowly.

"Very well, then — you shall go. But see to it that you return to us shortly!"

To be free again! With all speed, Handel made himself ready and was soon on his way in the lumbering coach — off to the beautiful country of England!

CHAPTER FOUR

A THICK BLANKET of fog had crept from the quiet hills into the lowlands, settling over all the countryside, swallowing the trees, the houses, and even the roadway as Handel watched from the coach window. Now and then he could hear the driver, urging the horses on through the gray curtain, step by step, mile after mile of the last lap of the journey from Hanover to the sea.

"Steady, Bess. Easy there, Tom. Scared of a little mist? But there's nothing to hurt you, my beauties."

It was late at night when they drew up at the old harbor inn that loomed suddenly out of the heavy fog. Sliding down from the high seat, the driver patted the horses kindly, and poking his head into the carriage, he called cheerily,

"Here we are, sir. And horses about finished."

"A long ride, driver."

"Considerable, sir. Considerable."

Stumbling out of the dark carriage, Handel listened eagerly to the low surging sounds that crept up through the mist. He was at the sea, and in the morning he would set sail for England! Turning to the door of the inn, he knocked loudly.

In a moment the great oaken door swung wide, and there stood the short, plump innkeeper in red flannel robe and nightcap, peering out into the darkness.

"Welcome, stranger," he cried heartily. Quickly leading the way to the back room, he fanned the glowing logs into a bright flame. "Supper in a moment, sir!"

How good it was to bask in the cheering warmth of the great open fire after the long ride from Hanover. Hungrily sniffing the round, juicy sausages, Handel watched the jolly innkeeper as he moved them from the flame, turning them now and then until at last they were done to a turn.

Never did a simple meal taste so good, and thanking the innkeeper warmly, he stumbled off to bed and was soon fast asleep, the wash of the ocean sounding in his ears.

All too soon the gray morning light found its way through the small porthole window, waking Handel with a start. It must be midmorning, and time for the boat to set sail for England!

It did not take him long to make himself ready, and hurrying to the landing, he looked out at the shining water where the little vessel lay in the sun, waiting calmly for her passengers.

Joyously going aboard, Handel looked around in surprise. But where were the other voyagers? Only a few sailors were about, busily scrubbing the decks in the slanting rays of the sun. Looking up from his work, one of the men smiled to see a passenger, ready to sail at sunup!

"Rather early to be about, sir."

"But I'm on my way to England!"

"Ship won't be sailing for a few hours, sir. Better go below and find a good place to sleep."

"Thank you, sailor."

But the time sped quickly by and when the few passengers were aboard, the gong sounded with a sharp clang and the little vessel headed out to sea, ploughing sturdily through the choppy waters.

Handel had never seen the ocean before and he leaned far over the railing where the spray could dash against his face and he could taste the salty brine on his lips.

As the hours rolled by, he wished that the voyage could go on and on, but in the distance was the shore, and soon it was time to land.

London at last! Yes, it was all as he had imagined it to be, with Westminster Abbey, old London Bridge, and Big Ben, booming the hour with measured stroke from the high clock tower overlooking the town.

But there was little time to enjoy the city, for as soon as it became known that the famous composer, Handel, was in London, invitations came to his door, begging him to conduct one of his operas for the people.

He would write them a new composition instead, and shutting himself away, Handel thought of nothing but the work before him, and in just two short weeks, the new opera, "Rinaldo" was completed. It was so filled with pure, glowing melody, it is no wonder that when it was given for the large, eager audience, rousing cheers rang throughout Queen's Hall.

"Bravo! Handel! Handel! Handel!"

In one night the opera became famous, and all London crowded to the theater in chairs and carriages, from dark lanes and byways, to hear the beautiful work. The name of Handel was spoken everywhere, and so many invitations came to his door to play in homes and churches and concert halls, that the master could only shake his head in wonder.

He liked the friendly English people and longed to make London his home. But there was little hope of his wish coming true, with the Prince of Hanover expecting him to return to his court very soon.

But Handel could not go yet — not when there was so much for him to do in the English capital. The weeks stretched into months and still he was too busy to leave.

One morning, as he sat at his work, a little group of dignified Englishmen stood at his door.

"Herr Handel, we have come to you in the name of our good Queen, who requests that you write a composition for the celebration of England's new peace treaty."

Handel listened breathlessly. This was a great honor, indeed!

"Thank you, gentlemen. I will be happy to carry out the wishes of the Queen of England."

Joyously Handel began the work and when the composition was finished, he sat at the organ in the vast St. Paul's Cathedral to lead the strong, stirring music before the many notables gathered there.

Queen Anne was so pleased with the service that Handel had rendered to England that the very next morning she sent a special messenger to his door with a heavy purse of gold and the promise that for every year spent in England, the composer would receive the sum of two hundred pounds.

Handel was overjoyed at his good fortune. Never had he been so rich before! Now he could buy himself a new coat, for he needed one badly. And it would be made by the finest tailor in all London, with the latest braiding and special gold buttons.

But very soon afterward, the good Queen died, and word was speedily sent to the Prince of Hanover, asking him to come to London at once, to be crowned the King of England.

The Prince of Hanover in England! Handel was worried, indeed, for he had been away from the court of Hanover far too long. The new King would be very angry, and was sure to mete out sound punishment to his concert master.

Suddenly an idea came to Handel. He would write some special music for the celebration, to serenade the new King on the River Thames. But there was all too little time, and setting to work with all his might, Handel finished the "Water Music" just as the special day arrived.

Quickly gathering his little band of musicians together, he hurried with them to the river, anxiously waiting for the King to appear. Suddenly a blast of trumpets sounded near the water's edge and there, leading the stately procession, was the new ruler, his jeweled robe shining in the moonlight. Making his way to the river, he slowly took his place in the velvet-lined barge.

"Quickly, men!" commanded Handel softly. "Into the barge with your instruments!"

Without a sound, the musicians took their places in the boat behind that of the King, and as the barges moved slowly down the river, the music began. The lovely, graceful melodies floated out over the water and a pleased smile stole over the face of the King. The English people had fine music in their country, indeed!

The charming pieces stopped for a moment and the monarch raised his hand.

"Tell the musicians to play that music again," he commanded, "and remind them not to miss a single note!"

At last the barges docked at Chelsea, where a fine supper awaited the royal company, and stepping ashore, the King spoke to one of his courtiers.

"Who in England has written this fine music?"

"The noted composer Handel, Your Majesty. And he has conducted it especially for your pleasure."

"Handel! Here? Bring the rascal to me at once!"

In a moment, Handel stood before the ruler of England.

"I humbly beseech your gracious pardon for not return-
ing earlier to the court of Hanover. It will not happen again,
Your Majesty."

A low chuckle sounded over his head.

"So! Then it is well that you have already chosen England
for your country, my fine concert master. But come, come,
Handel—all is forgiven. And now for your punishment you
shall play your music again while the company dines."

Breathing a sigh of joy, Handel turned to the men, and never was music played with more spirit! Especially this "Graceful Dance" that you will be eager to hear. Hasn't it a beautiful melody?

GRACEFUL DANCE
from the "Water Music"
(TRACK 9)

The next morning, when a messenger arrived at Handel's door bearing a scroll from the King, the composer tremblingly broke the heavy gold seal. Was his real punishment coming at last? Opening the paper, he read the words before him.

"George, King of England, hereby grants the composer, George Frederic Handel, the yearly sum of two hundred pounds, as long as he shall live in England, serving the King with his music."

Two hundred pounds a year! And still with another two hundred pounds for teaching the royal children, as well as the sum from Queen Anne, he would be as rich as a king!

And now for long years, Handel lived in London, writing operas and conducting them for the people. More than any place in all the world, Handel loved England, and the happiest day of his life came to him when he was made a citizen, which meant that from that day on, England would forever be his home.

At the invitation of the Duke of Chandos, Handel went to live at his princely mansion at Edgeware, to conduct the fine orchestra there. One morning he decided to take a long walk and explore the countryside, and striding over the broad fields, he was just entering Cannons when a crashing thunderstorm broke over his head.

The rain pounded on him furiously, and feeling his way along an old wall, he came to an open doorway. A shelter at last! Looking up, he found himself in a blacksmith's shop and there, before the blazing forge, a busy smithy in stout leather apron, was pounding on his anvil,  lustily singing an old folk melody.

With clothes dripping, Handel seated himself beside the glowing fire, smiling with delight as the song went on, its many verses seeming never to end. The lovely simple melody caught his fancy. Why, this tune could be made into a fine composition! Rising quickly, he nodded to the old smithy.

"Thank you for your kind shelter, sir."

"And right welcome you are, stranger."

Leaving the village behind him, Handel strode over the fields, heartily singing the smithy's song. Arriving at Edgeware, he sat at once to write the music that had worked itself out in his mind.

You must ask someone to play this delightful music at once!

THE HARMONIOUS BLACKSMITH
(TRACK 10)

119

And now all London was astir, for the opera house that had been closed for so long, was to be opened again. Of course no one but Handel should be the conductor, and to the composer at Edgeware, King George sent his fastest messenger, bidding him leave at once for Dresden, to select new singers there.

With all eagerness Handel set out in the coach, smiling to himself as he thought of a little surprise. He would stop in Halle for a visit with Mother Handel and Aunt Anna!

How could he ever wait to get there? The miles seemed never to end, but at last he rumbled into the little village and came to the cobblestoned street where he had played as a boy. Leaving the carriage, he ran to the old Schlamm House, his cries ringing out joyously.

"Mother! Aunt Anna!"

Two little old ladies hurried to the doorway, their white caps bobbing in the sun.

"George! At last you have come home to us! And now a great conductor and composer!" they went on breathlessly.

How good it was to be with his dear ones again! But the time with them was all too short and soon he was on his way again, waving good-byes from the coach window until the carriage turned at the end of the street.

Hardly had he left Halle than a stranger walked into the village, and stopping at the Schlamm House, rapped on the door with his stout cane. Perhaps George had come back again, thought Aunt Anna as she lifted the latch and peered out. But a stranger bowed to greet her, his black bowler hat under his arm.

"My name is Sebastian Bach, and I have heard that the great composer, Handel, is here in Halle. I have walked from Leipzig to see him."

"From Leipzig!" exclaimed Aunt Anna, wonderingly.

"All the way from Leipzig to see our Handel! But he is gone, sir. Only a few minutes ago did he leave in the coach."

A look of keen disappointment crossed the tired face of the great composer.

"Then I must start back to Leipzig at once, for my rascally choir boys will be getting into mischief without their Cantor." And putting his little bowler hat on his head, Bach strode away, his sturdy back disappearing at the end of the street.

Through the years that went swiftly by, more than forty operas came from Handel's pen, besides many songs and works for orchestra and for special instruments, as well. As soon as they were finished, they were carefully copied for the printers by the faithful Smith, so that everywhere, the people could have the beautiful works of the master to play and sing.

But now that he was growing older, Handel lived quietly in his tall stone house on Brook Street, giving concerts on the organ and composing. The people of London were always eager for new music and Handel decided to write an oratorio for them, music that would be performed in the church, with singers and chorus and an orchestra to accompany them.

The early sunlight flooded the front room of the Handel house as the master, his red morning coat carefully in place and his wig neatly tied, took his place at the oval wooden table, well supplied with pens and fresh paper by his good friend, Smith.

But the simple armchair was a bit too tight for the master, who was fast growing stout. Changing for a larger one, he smiled as melodies began to pour into his mind for his oratorio, the "Messiah."

Throughout the long day the notes flowed from his pen in a steady stream, and when darkness came to shut away the light from his paper, there was still no time for rest, for the music must go on.

Quietly lighting the candle, the servant brought fresh hot food, but Handel took no notice. Through the long night hours the scratching of his pen sounded through the bare rooms as the master labored on, his eyes glowing with a strange fire as the glorious music rang through his mind.

Then, when all London was waking to the new day, he took his dripping candle and climbing the broad stairs, fell wearily into bed.

On the twenty-fourth day the work was finished. Never before had such a giant task been accomplished. Sighing happily, Handel put down his pen.

"Smith! Smith!" he called. "Come quickly! My newest and dearest child is born."

The faithful copyist hurried to the master, and seeing tears on his cheek, stopped in surprise.

"Oh, Smith, such a beautiful time I have had with my 'Messiah.' The very gates of heaven seemed to open above me and as the music went onto the paper, choirs of angels with glad eyes sang the 'Hallelujah Chorus.'"

"It must be beautiful, indeed, master."

"You shall see, Smith, you shall see. But come now, make copies for the printers at once, and please, no mistakes!"

"I will watch carefully," answered the copyist, hurrying off to do his master's bidding. Then, turning back, he cautioned, "And while I make the copies, you must rest from your music, Master Handel."

A burst of laughter sounded through the room.

"Rest! But Smith — I rest only in my music!" And reaching for fresh paper, the master began a new oratorio!

A few days later, as Handel sat at his little harpsichord, playing a part of his new work, a messenger arrived at his door. Opening the carefully written scroll, Handel read:

> "The Lord-Lieutenant of Ireland humbly beseeches the famous English composer, George Frederic Handel, to grant the people of Ireland the honor of a visit to their country, to perform for them his noble compositions."

Handel looked up with a bright smile. A new adventure was calling him. How he did love adventures!

"Pack at once!" he commanded. "I am off for Ireland. And Smith — get word to my singers to meet me in Dublin. I shall need them there."

What a time the two servants had, getting the master ready! And hovering about, Handel watched the packing with anxious eye.

"The ruffles, my good man — watch the ruffles! And that is my newest velvet coat. Handle it with great care!"

At last the bulging bags were tied and Handel was off in the coach. Arriving in Chester, he made his way to the Golden Falcon, for heavy seas were running in the channel and the packet boats had long been delayed.

This would be a good time to rehearse the chorus parts of the new oratorio, and from the church near by, the choir boys hastened to the little inn, eager to perform for the noted master.

"Now then, my fine young singers, can you read this music at sight?"

"Oh yes, sir."

"Very well," answered Handel, giving them the sheets of the "Messiah." "I will accompany you. Now then, begin!"

Haltingly the boys started, but after a few quavering notes, there was dead silence. Handel looked up in amusement.

"But you told me that you could read at sight!"

"Oh yes, sir, but not at *first* sight."

In a few days the sea was calm enough to board the packet boat and soon Handel found himself in the Irish countryside, fresh and sparkling and green. News spread quickly of the arrival of the noted master, and throughout Dublin, honors were showered upon him and visitors crowded to his door, eager to catch a glimpse of the famous composer.

At last the rehearsals for the oratorio were finished and the great day arrived for the performance of the "Messiah."

All Dublin was astir for the greatest event ever to take place in that city, and in order to have room enough for the people, a request was sent far and wide, asking,

"The favour of the Ladies not to come with hoops this day to the Music Hall in Fishamble Street. The Gentlemen are desired to come without their swords."

Handel, in his fine new costume of deep green velvet, was pleased with the vast audience that listened wide-eyed to such music as had never before been heard in Dublin. They would never forget this day.

At the end of a year with the warm-hearted people of Ireland, Handel returned to England, happier than he had been for many long years. The English people welcomed him back and at once begged him to honor them with a performance of the "Messiah" which had won such fame in Ireland.

Straight to the opera house went the tireless master and when all was in readiness for a performance of his greatest work, Handel seated himself at the organ. But as he started to give the signal for the music to begin, his ear caught the sound of whispering and down came his hand.

"Hush! Hush!" whispered one of the royal ladies in the King's box. "Can you not see? Handel is angry!"

The audience, as well, had noticed the trembling wig of the master and at once there was silence. Then, putting his hands on the keys, Handel began to play and in awe, the people listened to the noble work with its triumphant "Hallelujah Chorus," telling that the Christ would live forever as King of Kings and Lord of Lords.

The King was so deeply stirred with the exultant music, that when the first Hallelujah rang through the hall, he rose to his feet and remained standing until the last note of the chorus echoed through the house.

This first part of the glorious Hallelujah Chorus you may be able to sing while someone plays the accompaniment.

HALLELUJAH CHORUS
(TRACK 11)

One day, after the master had conducted his favorite oratorio at the Foundling Hospital to raise funds for the homeless children sheltered there, he stopped on his way home to speak with his old friend, Lord Kinnoul.

"Ah, Handel! Handel! This "Messiah" of yours is setting the world on fire. It is fine entertainment, indeed!"

"Entertainment!" exclaimed the master, his wig shaking violently. "I do not wish to entertain you, sir, but to make you better!"

Poor Handel! His eyes that had served him so long and so well, began to trouble him. They smarted and ached whenever he tried to write and he decided to ask the King's doctor to come to see him at once. Word was sent with all haste to the palace and soon the tall, handsome Doctor Taylor arrived at the house on Brook Street, examining the anxious master with the greatest care.

"Ah, my good Handel," sighed the noted doctor, "I must tell you that there is little that can be done for your trouble. I am sorry, sir."

A wave of deep sadness crept into the heart of the master. To spend the rest of his days in darkness? And not to be able to see to write his melodies? Then he must work at once, while there was yet time.

Hurrying to the little table he seized his pen and the notes poured onto the paper before him. Faster, faster, while there was yet time! Now the music of the oratorio, "Jeptha," written to Morrell's words, was beginning to sing!

But in the struggling days that followed, there were many sad times when Handel could not see. Closer and still closer he bent his head until his eyes were almost touching the paper. As the last notes came from his pen, someone entered the room.

"Morrell! It is good of you to come. And see — the oratorio, "Jeptha," is just finished — my music written for your words. They are your best, my friend."

"My poor words are honored with such noble music, sir," answered the little minister kindly. "And I will write more if you wish, and Smith, here, can take down the notes as you tell them to him."

A light of joy broke like a ray of sunshine over the face of the master.

"Then I can still sing my songs for England! England — how I love her!"

Through the days that went quietly by, the faithful Smith sat with Handel, carefully putting down the notes of a composition as they came from the master's lips. Then, when the work was finished, Handel listened closely as the music was played for him. But sadly he shook his head.

"No, no Smith — what I long to say is not there. We will try again, just once more, yes?"

As the darkness came to shut away the last ray of light, the heart of the master became ever more lonely. But no matter how great his suffering, no one must know. Happily he welcomed his close friends and on calm sunny days, rowed with them on the River Thames, peacefully smoking his long pipe.

Alone in his house at night when he could not sleep, Handel felt his way to his beloved harpsichord, to play in the stillness, parts of his music that he loved best. Softly the melodies stole to the far corners of the little house, or marched triumphantly up the broad staircase, echoing in grandeur through the halls.

Then, strangely comforted, he stole away to bed and to sleep.

His concerts for the people never stopped. With head erect, he sat at the organ, playing his works from memory or making entire compositions as he went along while in wonder and awe, the people listened to the Father of the Oratorio, one of the greatest composers and organists that the world has ever known.

When the last notes had died away, the audience rose to honor their noble musician.

"Long live our great master! Long live our Handel!"
echoed their cries.

And so the little boy from the village of Halle, who loved
music so much that he stole away at night to the attic to
learn by himself how to play, grew to be the greatest
musician of all England, the beloved George Frederic
Handel, honored through his whole life long at the Court
of Kings.

And here you will find more beautiful music that Handel wrote: delightful minuets and gavottes and sonatinas that you will want to play. And how you will enjoy listening to more of the tuneful melodies from the "Water Music," while someone plays them for you over and over again, for we can never hear enough of Handel's glorious music.

MINUET

(TRACK 12)

BOURRÉE

COURANTE

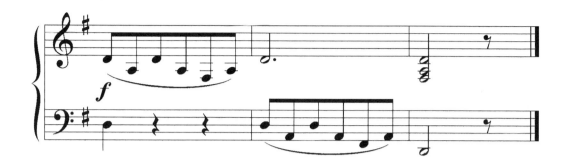

MINUET
(TRACK 15)

144

PASSEPIED
(TRACK 16)

MINUET
[from "Samson"]
(TRACK 17)

PRELUDE

MINUET

(TRACK 19)

149

FUGUE

(TRACK 20)

HORNPIPE

from the "Water Music"

Allegro

CHACONNE

(TRACK 22)

Variation II

Variation III

Variation IV

BOURRÉE
from the "Water Music"

(TRACK 23)

INTERMEZZO
(TRACK 24)

159

GAVOTTE

(TRACK 25)

FUGHETTA

(TRACK 26)

SONATINA

(TRACK 27)

Allegro

LARGO

(TRACK 28)